T0413371

AMAZING MIGRATIONS

ON THE MOVE WITH MONARCH BUTTERFLIES

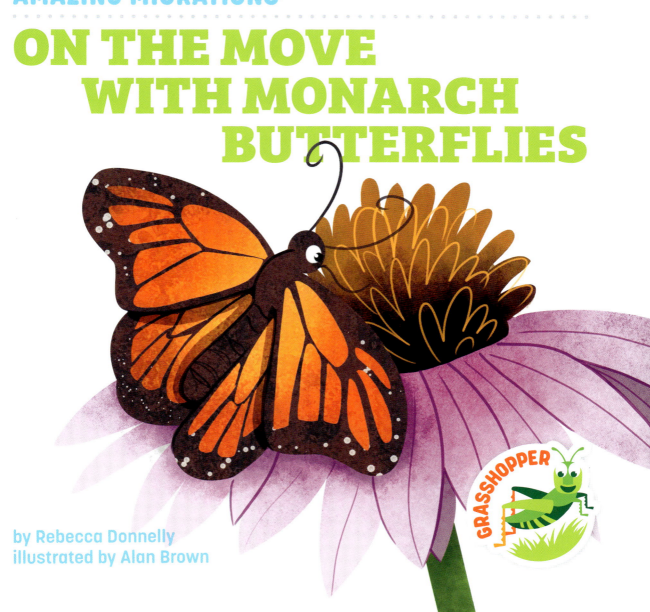

by Rebecca Donnelly
illustrated by Alan Brown

GRASSHOPPER

Tools for Parents & Teachers

Grasshopper Books enhance imagination and introduce the earliest readers to fiction with fun storylines and illustrations. The easy-to-read text supports early reading experiences with repetitive sentence patterns and sight words.

Before Reading

- Discuss the cover illustration. What do readers see?
- Look at the glossary together. Discuss the words.

Read the Book

- Read the book to the child, or have him or her read independently.
- "Walk" through the book and look at the illustrations. Who is the main character? What is happening in the story?

After Reading

- Prompt the child to think more. Ask: Miles and his generation live for eight months. The other generations live for only a few weeks. How does Miles survive so much longer?

Grasshopper Books are published by Jump!
5357 Penn Avenue South
Minneapolis, MN 55419
www.jumplibrary.com

Library of Congress Cataloging-in-Publication Data

Names: Donnelly, Rebecca, author.
Brown, Alan, illustrator.
Title: On the move with monarch butterflies
Rebecca Donnelly; illustrated by Alan Brown.
Description: Minneapolis, MN: Jump!, Inc., [2023]
Series: Amazing migrations | Includes index.
Audience: Ages 7–10
Identifiers: LCCN 2021060816 (print)
LCCN 2021060817 (ebook)
ISBN 9781636908915 (hardcover)
ISBN 9781636908922 (paperback)
ISBN 9781636908939 (ebook)
Subjects: LCSH: Monarch butterfly–Migration–Juvenile literature.
Migratory animals–Juvenile literature.
Classification: LCC QL561.N9 D66 2023 (print)
LCC QL561.N9 (ebook)
DDC 595.78/9–dc23/eng/20220110
LC record available at https://lccn.loc.gov/2021060816
LC ebook record available at https://lccn.loc.gov/2021060817

Editor: Eliza Leahy
Direction and Layout: Anna Peterson
Illustrator: Alan Brown

Printed in the United States of America at Corporate Graphics in North Mankato, Minnesota.

Table of Contents

A Long Way to Fly

Hello! I'm Miles. Two days ago, I hatched from my egg on this milkweed plant in southern Canada.

I'm a caterpillar now, but soon I'll be a monarch butterfly. I started eating right away. Milkweed is all I eat. I need lots of energy for my metamorphosis. That is how I turn into a butterfly!

I eat and grow for two weeks. I molt four times. I grow new, bigger skin each time. Then I hang upside down! I'll molt once more.

Do you like my new green skin? It's called a chrysalis. I'll hang here for two more weeks.

chrysalis ·····▶

Now look at me! With these wings, I will fly nearly 3,000 miles (4,828 kilometers) to Mexico. I will spend winter there.

Four generations of monarchs are born every year, but only the last generation makes this long migration. That's me!

It is August. Time for us to fly south!
It takes a lot of work to fly that far.
We fly on air currents to help.

We drink nectar along the way.
We store energy for the long winter!

13

We made it! We'll spend winter in this fir tree forest in central Mexico. We cluster in tree branches to stay warm. We go dormant for most of the winter to save energy. That's how we can live so much longer than other generations. See you in spring!

In spring, the sun gets stronger. We start to fly and look for water and nectar before flying back north. I find water in this puddle!

egg

We mate as we fly north. Females lay eggs on the undersides of milkweed leaves. This hides them from predators like spiders, ants, and ladybugs. Females usually lay one egg at a time. Each female will lay hundreds of eggs in her lifetime!

We keep flying and leave the eggs. After they hatch, the caterpillars will go through metamorphosis like I did! Then they will fly north, too.

The first, second, and third generations will only live for a few weeks. They will mate and lay their own eggs. The fourth will live for more than eight months, like me!

We've flown more than 1,000 miles (1,609 km)! It's time for me to stop. My children and grandchildren will continue. They will spread out across the United States. My great-grandchildren will fly south, like I did.

I might be a tiny insect, but my life was a big adventure!

Migration Map

Many monarch butterflies spend winter in Mexico, like Miles. Others go to Florida or California. Take a look at different monarchs' migrations!

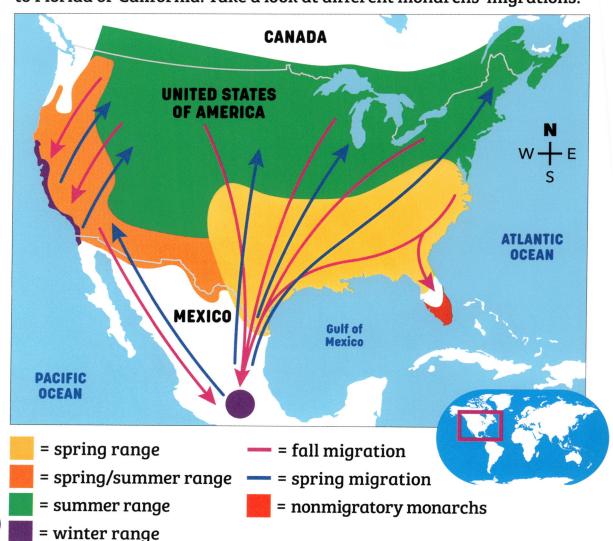

- = spring range
- = spring/summer range
- = summer range
- = winter range
- = fall migration
- = spring migration
- = nonmigratory monarchs

Let's Review!

Why do Miles and his friends migrate south for winter?

A. to stay warm   **B.** to find food   **C.** to mate   **D.** to raise young

Glossary

air currents: Movements of air in the atmosphere.

chrysalis: The hard outer skin of a caterpillar as it turns into an adult butterfly.

cluster: To form a group close together.

dormant: Temporarily slowed down or inactive, like in a deep sleep.

energy: The ability or strength to do things without getting tired.

generations: All members of a group born around the same time.

mate: To join together to produce young.

metamorphosis: A series of changes caterpillars go through as they develop into adults.

migration: The movement of animals from one area to another.

molt: To lose old skin so that new skin can grow.

nectar: A sweet liquid in flowers that attracts pollinators.

predators: Animals that hunt other animals for food.

Let's Review! Answer Key: **A.** to stay warm

23

Index

To Learn More

FACT SURFER

Finding more information is as easy as 1, 2, 3.

❶ Go to www.factsurfer.com

❷ Enter "**onthemovewithmonarchbutterflies**" into the search box.

❸ Choose your book to see a list of websites.